NOW THAT *you* are BORN AGAIN

Scriptures taken from the Holy Bible, New International Version®, NIV®. Copyright © 1973, 1978, 1984, 2011 by Biblica, Inc.™ Used by permission of Zondervan. All rights reserved worldwide. www.zondervan.com The "NIV" and "New International Version" are trademarks registered in the United States Patent and Trademark Office by Biblica, Scripture quotations taken from the (NASB®) New American Standard Bible®, Copyright © 1960, 1971, 1977, 1995, 2020 by The Lockman Foundation. Used by permission. All rights reserved. www.lockman.org. Inc.™ The Holy Bible, English Standard Version® (ESV®) Copyright © 2001 by Crossway, a publishing ministry of Good News Publishers. All rights reserved. ESV Text Edition: 2016. Scripture taken from the New King James Version®. Copyright © 1982 by Thomas Nelson. Used by permission. All rights reserved.

This manuscript has undergone viable editorial work and proofreading, yet human limitations may have resulted in minor grammatical or syntax-related errors remaining in the finished book. The understanding of the reader is requested in these cases. While precaution has been taken in the preparation of this book, the publisher and author assume no responsibility for errors or omissions, or for damages resulting from the use of the information contained herein.

Content editing provided by Caroline Horner and Kate Powell.

This book is set in the typeface *Athelas* designed by Veronika Burian and Jose Scaglione.

Developed in Partnership with *Tall Pine Books*
119 E Center Street, Suite B4A | Warsaw, Indiana 46580
www.tallpinebooks.com

| 1 22 22 20 16 02 |

Published in the United States of America

NOW THAT *you* *are* BORN AGAIN

DISCOVER *the* JOY *of* GROWING UP INTO SALVATION

PETER K. LOUIS

"Like a new building, a new believer needs a strong foundation to undergird and provide a base for their new spiritual life. In *Now That You Are Born Again*, my friend Peter Louis provides foundational truths for believers to grow and mature in their faith."

—JOHN BEVERE
Best-selling Author and Minister
Co-founder of *Messenger International* & *MessengerX*

"Peter Louis is an amazing man of God! He is an amazing teacher as well, with a true pastoral heart for the bride. This book gives hands-on keys for what to do once you're saved. It is one of the most incredible processes to dive into. Discipleship is at the heart of the message of the glorious Gospel! The good news!"

—TODD WHITE
Founder and President of *Lifestyle Christianity*

"*Now That You are Born Again* authored by Peter Louis is a must read for laying the foundation for a long and joyous relationship for new believers. I personally want it in the hands of every new believer in our ministry! It's a must-read book with the potential to anchor your faith in truth!"

—T.D. JAKES SR.
The Potter's House of Dallas

CONTENTS

GOD'S DESIGN
for YOUR LIFE

JESUS IS FASCINATING. He's more beautiful, kind, loving, joyful, pure, and majestic than we could ever comprehend and yet He has invited you to *intimately know him*. He has welcomed you with open arms into the family of God. He's made a way for you to be born again! Welcome to the greatest, most exhilarating journey of your life.

If you've recently given your life to Jesus Christ, or you've grown up in church and have rededicated your life to God or maybe you just recently heard the gospel of Jesus Christ and surrendered to his call, I wrote this book just for you. Christianity can seem confusing with so many different denominations and expressions of the Christian faith. So what should you focus on?

You may be asking questions like...

What does it really mean to be born again?

What does a life of following Jesus look like?

How do I know if I'm in a healthy spiritual environment?

What should I focus on as a Christian, and what is my ultimate purpose?

These are really important questions to answer as you begin this beautiful, adventure-filled spiritual journey with God. I aim to answer these seemingly big questions with simple, true answers that will transform your walk with God and therefore your life.

For instance, if you don't know what Jesus meant when he said, "*You must be born again,*" then you will not be able to fully enjoy your spiritual journey. You will strive constantly, in one way or another, to find affection and love from your Father instead of enjoying it every step of the way regardless of where you are in your spiritual maturity.

If you don't know what a life of following Jesus looks like, you might stop following him when life gets hard. Without a healthy perspective on the trials in your life, you might think that something is wrong with you or worse...with God!

How do you know if you're in a healthy spiritual environment? The answers to this question are so important for you to enjoy this new life in God. Unfortunately the world, and sadly sometimes even churches, do not provide a healthy spiritual environment to grow in. You need to know how to find and cultivate a healthy spiritual environment so you can grow up into all that God has called you to!

Finally, what is your ultimate purpose in being a Christian? Do you know the end from the beginning? If not, you might get lost along the way! If you don't know where you're going, how will you know which turns to take?

Sadly, many believers set off on their spiritual journey without this knowledge of God. They have ventured off into the wilderness and continue to wander without growing, without peace, without power, and without purpose.

YOU WILL NOT WANDER!

You have been born again, you've surrendered to Jesus, and now you are going to enter into an abundant and meaningful Christian life. You are entering into the greatest adventure with the greatest God with the greatest love for you! You were born (again) at just the right time!

The days of wandering, confusion about the Christian faith, and offense at everything and everyone are over! The days of powerlessness are over. The days of anxiety and fear are over. The days of bondage are over.

The greatest privilege ever offered to humanity is the gift of being born into the family of God. You have been given the right to become a child of God (John 1:12-

13), and God has become your very own Father through his son Jesus Christ (1 John 3:1). As a good Father, he has *designed* a life for you that is filled with peace, joy, purpose, and pleasure!

It is **God's design** that holds the secret to this beautiful life. God is the Maker of the heavens and the earth and all that is in them (Psalm 146:6) which means that we must study carefully how God has designed his creation to grow! The Bible says, *"He chose to give us birth through the word of truth, that we might be a kind of first-fruits of all he created"* (James 1:18). So you, as one who has been born again through the Word of truth (the Gospel), have become a new creation. You are a new species! His Word says again, *"Therefore, if anyone is in Christ, he is a new creature. The old has passed away; behold the new has come"* (2 Corinthians 5:17).

And every one of God's creations grows in the same simple way! There are five key elements of God's design that are required for any one of God's creations to grow, including Christians! The five elements are...

1. A good seed
2. A healthy environment
3. Nourishment
4. Time
5. Fulfillment of purpose

Let's take a look at my Texas garden for a good example. If I take a healthy jalapeño seed (#1 *a good seed)* and I plant it in rich, fertile soil (#2 *environment*) and I give it enough water, sunlight, and air (#3 *nourishment*) in the right amount of time (#4 *time)* it will begin to grow. The growth may appear slowly at the beginning because the initial growth happens beneath the soil, hidden from sight. But when all of God's elements are in place, time becomes our friend and growth above the soil is inevitable. When the right amount of time has passed, assuming the other three elements have been in place, you will have a healthy jalapeño plant bearing beautiful, ripe jalapeños, which is the fulfillment of its purpose (#5 *purpose).*

Understanding these five key elements and how they all work together is foundational for your spiritual journey. Once you are familiar with God's design for spiritual growth and life, you will discover that growing up in God is a great joy! It will almost feel as though it is TOO GOOD to be true! How will you know whether or not there is mature growth in your spiritual life? What are the things we should be looking for along the way? What should you expect to see as you continue in the faith?

As you grow up into salvation (1 Peter 2:2) you will start seeing three distinct signs of spiritual growth. These three "fruits" are a sign that you are actually growing up into Christ!

- <u>You will find lasting freedom from sin</u> – This freedom will look like old thought patterns and sinful habits becoming powerless. Growing up into salvation looks like freedom from sin!

- <u>Deeper intimacy and confidence with God</u> – One of the sure signs you are growing up into salvation is *peace* and *confidence with God*. Many Christians are not confident in their position before God. As a result they don't live at peace with God and find it hard to enjoy intimacy with him.

- <u>You will begin to love like Jesus</u> – One of the greatest privileges of being born again and growing up into salvation is the joy of sharing the love of God with the world around you. As you grow up into salvation you will discover the joy and power of loving like Jesus! This includes radical forgiveness, humble serving, steadfast patience, ridiculous kindness, mind-blowing power, and deliverance and life-giving wisdom flowing through your life.

This is the purpose of this book and the desire of my heart. I want you to discover that belonging to Jesus Christ is the highest and most rewarding calling that anyone could ever have. You have been invited into union with Christ. You're now being transformed into his image for the purpose of showing those around you what He is really like! You're born again into the Kingdom of God. With that new-found identity, let's dive into each of these five elements and discover the joy of growing up into God.

CHAPTER ONE

YOU'RE A GOOD SEED

THERE ARE MANY Christians that still believe they are a *bad seed*. A Christian life rooted in a bad seed mentality can quickly lead to shame, guilt, frustration, confusion, self-loathing, and a lifetime of striving to overcome the badness inside. It's easy to see why the bad seed mentality has such a hold on Christians. Because they grew up in sin and became accustomed to being enslaved to selfish desires and earthly passions, when those feelings or thoughts surface *after* surrendering their life to Christ they assume there is still something wrong at the seed level. What do I mean? The assumption is that the presence of sinful desires and actions speaks to our identity.

But as we will discover, if a born-again believer still believes they are a sinner (a bad seed) then you will never be able to grow up into salvation! Imagine a friend of yours showed you a rotten apple seed and told you he was going to try to grow an apple tree. Imagine he was well versed in the type of soil and ideal conditions an apple seed needs to grow and could perfectly articulate the process to you. But if the seed is rotten, none of that matters! You cannot grow up into salvation and maintain the belief that you are a bad seed!

What happens inside our own heads matters. Our thought life matters. So the first thing you must understand and reorient your mind to is that as a believer in Jesus Christ, when you repented from your sins and surrendered your heart to Jesus, you became a **brand-new creation**! Read that again. You are a brand-new creation. YOU.

God doesn't just put bandages on the broken places in our lives; he makes them brand new! In other words, you are a good seed! And a good, healthy seed, planted in the right environment, will grow! We will describe a healthy spiritual environment in the next chapter, but for now we must establish the fact that through Christ **you have become a good seed!**

<u>Now that you're born again, look at what God says about you!</u>

YOU'RE A NEW CREATION! YOU ARE IN CHRIST! THE OLD HAS GONE!

*Therefore, if anyone is in Christ, the **new creation** has come: The **old has gone**, the new is here (2 Corinthians 5:17, NIV, emphasis added)!*

YOU'VE BEEN BORN OF GOD!

*Yet to all who did receive him, to those who believed in his name, he gave the right to become children of God—children born not of natural descent, nor of human decision or a husband's will, but **born of God** (John 1:12-13, NIV, emphasis added).*

YOU HAVE ESCAPED THE CORRUPTION IN THE WORLD AND BECOME A PARTAKER OF THE DIVINE NATURE!

*Through these he has given us his very great and precious promises, so that through them you may **participate in the divine nature**, having escaped the corruption in the world caused by evil desires (2 Peter 1:4, NIV, emphasis added).*

Can I recommend something to you? When your feet hit the floor each morning, read these verses over yourself. Remind yourself that you're a new creation, born of God, a partaker in the divine nature. You'll see a radical shift in your spiritual, mental, emotional, and even physical self.

One of the words the Bible uses to describe this good seed, your new nature in Christ, is *righteous*. **Righteousness is the state of being right before God.** It doesn't initially mean that you are doing all the right things; it means that you have *become* right. It means that God removes all that wasn't right with you and in you and he makes you right *in His son*.

The state of being righteous before God will produce a lasting peace that no one or circumstance can ever take away. If you're right with God, the impact of the world on you goes to zero. Stressful day on the job? You're right with God. Strained relationships? You're right with God. Fear over the future? You're right with God. The purpose of this chapter is to make you confident that you are a good seed and that you have become the righteousness of God in Christ Jesus (2 Corinthians 5:21). Jesus became our sin so we could become the righteousness of God.

Now, let's consider a newborn baby. As newborns, we don't immediately start *doing* sinful things like murdering, gossiping, stealing, lusting, and coveting other people's stuff...it is the same when we are born again. We become spiritual infants where our righteousness, though in seed form, requires a healthy environment, nourishment, and time to fully grow up. Make no mistake; the gift of righteousness given to us in Christ is not tied to our behavior. But it will eventually transform our behavior into righteous living. More on that later.

One of the biggest reasons so many Christians fail to fully enjoy and thrive in their relationship with Jesus is that *they still believe they are a bad seed. In other words, they believe they are still "from Adam."* Let's unpack this expression...what do I mean when I say "from Adam"?

The Bible says, *"Therefore, just as sin came into the world through one man, and death through sin, and so death spread to all men because all sinned—"* (Romans 5:12, NIV), which means sin and death came to you and me through Adam. This is not good news. In fact, it seems really unfair. Why am I being punished for someone else's sin way back in the Garden of Eden? Before we get too far down this road of apparent "injustice," this question is quickly offset by the fact that Jesus Christ came to satisfy the wages of sin on our behalf (death) and freely offers us his life in return. That too is not fair! It is not fair that the perfect, sinless son of God suffered and died on a cross. The Christian faith will cause us to rethink what we know about justice and what we *think* is fair.

To believe we are "from Adam" is to believe we are bad seeds. It is to associate with the sin, brokenness, and death we inherited through Adam. A bad seed will always produce bad fruit. Jesus said it like this, "A good tree cannot bear bad fruit, and a bad tree cannot bear good fruit" (Matthew 7:18, NIV). A good tree cannot bear bad fruit because it is good! A bad tree or a bad seed cannot bear good fruit because it is bad!

To believe we are "from Adam" is to say things like...

"Well, we're only human."

"We will all continue to struggle with sin until Jesus comes back."

"I'm just a sinner."

We believe we are bad seeds or we are "from Adam" when we continue to embrace all the thoughts, feelings, and desires we had before we were born again. It is believing that judgmental, hateful, angry, prideful, lustful, anxious thoughts are still a *part of who we are*. If we believe this, defeat is certain. We cannot identify as bad seeds and grow up into salvation. The challenge we face here is that so many of us will continue to have certain thoughts, feelings, and desires we've had our whole lives. When these thoughts, feelings, and desires crop up, we immediately, almost unconsciously assume it's because we are *from Adam*.

Let me give you an example plucked from my own life. For years of my Christian life I wrestled with lustful thoughts. Eventually, I became addicted to pornography. My view of myself, women, and sexuality became skewed. The seed of sin that once took root in my heart produced in me all kinds of unholy behavior. Unfortunately, I was mistakenly taught that we as men would always struggle with masturbation and pornography. And as a result, I continued to identify all the lustful thoughts, desires, and actions as my own.

The devastating result of this mindset is that I quickly was filled with guilt, shame, and condemnation. Because I continued to struggle week after week with lustful thoughts and bouts of pornography addiction, I assumed my inability to find freedom was my own fault. Maybe I didn't really want to be free? Maybe I wasn't as close to God as I thought I was? Do I need more accountability? Do I need to read my Bible more? Maybe I was a bad seed after all? I was bombarded with questions, uncertainty, and insecurity in the wake of my ongoing sin struggles.

Over the years I've learned I'm not the only one who gets stuck in this cycle. I still regularly encounter Christians who are struggling with sin, longing for freedom, but not knowing what to do. It doesn't matter what the struggle is, it almost certainly originates from the sinful tendencies we inherited through Adam. And if we do not know the truth, that comes to us through the Gospel, through Jesus, we will spend years of our Christian life wrestling with a sinful identity that Jesus has already crucified on the cross.

I cannot overemphasize how important it is, as you begin this journey with God, that you begin to renew your mind to the beautiful, blood-bought truth that you are BORN AGAIN, a brand-new, good seed! The *only* way we will find lasting freedom from sin (thoughts, deeds, and desires) is to allow the Holy Spirit to renew our minds to the fact that we have been crucified with Christ, our old man has been buried with him, and our new self has been resurrected with Christ to newness of life.

So what do we do, as new creations, believers in Jesus Christ, if we encounter those old thoughts, struggles, and feelings we had before we were saved? We must be equipped with a revelation of Christ to know which path to take.

There are two roads you can travel. The first road is one that is a well-worn path. It is the road we learned to walk as children, the road Adam has walked a thousand miles. It is the road that serves our flesh, causes pain, and is marked by self-serving thoughts and desires. It is the road that gratifies our own sinful flesh. It is the road of offense, unforgiveness, anger, lust, comparison, anxiety, fear, and the list goes on. The temptation to travel this path lies in how frequently we have been down the path. We know the way so it is a strangely comfortable choice.

But now that you're born again, there is a better way!

The second road is the road of the Spirit. This is the new, but ancient way! Your flesh has never been this way before...until now. You must be taught and instructed how to walk in the Spirit. If you are not taught to walk in the Spirit you will simply default to traveling the path of Adam you have always known. But now that you are born again, we get to learn to walk in the Spirit. Though it may feel scary at first, walking in the Spirit will become as natural as the old path of Adam used to be.

When you come to the inevitable crossroad, your first step is the *most important*. Picture in your mind a crossroad in your life. You come upon it. Same old feelings, thoughts, and desires, and you're tempted to go down the old path and yield to them...as you always have. It could be any of the old desires and feelings you were never created for: fear, anxiety, loneliness, rejection, lust, anger, or pride. I'm naming them because it is important for you to know that these feelings and thoughts are not from Christ. The first temptation is to believe that these desires or feelings are still a part of who you are. Because you have known them, they feel like familiar friends. But the beauty and power of the Gospel is the proclamation of a new creation in Christ! The first step to walking in the Spirit is to be reminded that your sins, sinful nature, and old man were crucified on a cross and buried 2,000 years ago with Christ. This is the first, most important step at each of your crossroads.

STEP 1:
YOUR OLD MAN IS DEAD *and* POWERLESS

I have been crucified with Christ (Galatians 2:20) – When Paul says "I" he is referring to his old man. He's referring to everything he inherited from Adam. Every sinful thought, deed, and desire has been crucified *with Christ*. That is the key.

How can we who died to sin still live in it? (Romans 6:2-4) – Do you not know that all of us who have been baptized into Christ Jesus were baptized into his death? We were buried therefore with him by baptism into death, in order that, just as Christ was raised from the dead by the glory of the Father, we too might walk in newness of life.

For one who has died has been set free from sin (Romans 6:7) – The first step of walking in the Spirit is embracing the truth that our old man is dead.

So you also must consider yourselves dead to sin and alive to God in Christ Jesus (Romans 6:11) – Here the message is yet again: the first step of walking in the Spirit is to consider yourself (and all of its desires and feelings) dead to sin and alive to God in Christ Jesus.

Do you see how Step 1 is a battle of your mental state and thought life? What we think about ourselves matters in the Kingdom. What we think about Jesus' work on the cross matters. As believers in Jesus, our thoughts and beliefs are brand new. We are dead to sin because of what Jesus did. Say it over and over again until your mind learns, embraces, and believes this new and beautiful truth.

Now, I'm aware there is another side of this coin. Let's face it head-on.

A Christian might say or think: I'm certainly not dead to this thing (fill in the sinful thought or desire) because I feel it alive in me!

But I have good news. That is simply your flesh talking! We are so accustomed to walking in the flesh that we are sometimes offended at the thought of walking in the Spirit. The solution to battling your flesh? Step 1. Say it again with me: my old man was crucified with Christ. And now, we are ready for Step 2.

STEP 2:
YOU ARE ALIVE TO GOD *in* CHRIST JESUS

If the first step is considering yourself dead to sin...then the second step is considering yourself alive to God in Christ Jesus. To be dead to sin is to turn away from the path of the flesh, yet to be alive to God in Christ Jesus is to take a step towards the path of life! **Alive to God. You are alive to God. I am alive to God. Our brothers and sisters in Jesus are ALIVE TO GOD. It means we have access to the things of God. Peace, compassion, forgiveness, joy, rest, patience, love, power, purity. This, my friends, is the best good news!**

Let's look at an example. Let's imagine that you are struggling with fear and anxiety. Your crossroads might look like this. You find yourself feeling fearful and filled with anxiety. It could be about a relationship or your finances or your future. You are familiar with the anxiety landscape in the flesh, your old man: panic, worry, shortness of breath, the temptation to isolate and hide from others. The old way is what you know; it is familiar. And it doesn't work.

> "To be dead to sin is to turn away from the path of the flesh, yet to be alive to God in Christ Jesus is to take a step towards the path of life!"

But there's a new way now. You call to remembrance the moment you surrendered your life to Jesus and put your faith in him. You remember at once that the old you that was prone to fear and worry was nailed to Jesus on the cross. That old person has died. Though you feel fearful now, it must be because you are looking at the flesh or you are looking at some earthly situation. As you return to the moment you were born again, you discover that your old man is dead. You begin to consider yourself dead to fear because of the wonderful sacrifice and work of Jesus on the cross. You also consider that you are no longer obligated to be afraid of anything because the temptation to fear was not only crucified to a cross—it was buried in a grave!

Step 1 has been taken. Good! Now what? Each step you take is crucial because you are maintaining the faith of the Gospel, the belief that you are in fact a new creation.

All right—here comes Step 2 in our example. **You must start to consider yourself alive to God in Christ Jesus.** What does this mean? Well, if you are *in Christ Jesus,* that means he has given you access to his nature and likeness. What is Jesus like? Is he fearful? Does he worry about finances? If not, what does he do with all of his time? Instead of being fearful, what is he actually like? If you do not immediately know what Christ is like here, you might want to ask a believing friend, a spiritual mentor, or grab your Bible and flip to Matthew, Mark, Luke, or John. This part of your spiritual walk is really important. **In order to walk in the Spirit and enjoy our new life in Christ, we must know what he is really like!**

For this example I can tell you that Jesus is someone who completely trusts in His Father. He did not fear (and does not fear) when he walked this earth because of his deep trust and dependence upon the Father. Do you know what that means? **It means that in *Christ Jesus* you are invited to consider yourself *alive to God* in the same way.** Therefore, you do not have to fear because you have deep trust and dependence on God. It starts by allowing the Holy Spirit to renew your mind, and it is established as you put these things upon your lips in prayer.

"Father, thank you that I am dead to fear, worry, and anxiety. I thank you for the work of Jesus in forgiving me for all of the times I have doubted you and questioned your love for me. I'm so grateful that I don't have to try and overcome these things. You've already defeated them. Even though I am tempted to fear, I know that Jesus has saved me!

Thank you for placing me in Christ! Thank you that I am a good son (or daughter) who trusts you with my finances, my relationships, and my future. I trust you, Father, to care for me and all of my needs. I am alive to you! I am alive to your love and your faithfulness! Thank you that I have not been given a spirit of fear but of power, love, and a sound mind."

The wonderful thing about walking in the Spirit is that it is **simple**. It only requires two steps, repeated over and over, to make progress. And these are the only two steps you must learn to take if you want to walk in the Spirit. You must first consider yourself dead to sin (to Adam) and then you must consider yourself alive to God in Christ Jesus.

This process works no matter what you are going through. But, just like walking, if you fail to take one of the steps you will certainly stumble! This is why the

Bible says the righteous shall live by faith. It is only *by faith* that you will experience the freedom, peace, and confidence of being a new, righteous son or daughter before God.

Before we move on to the next chapter, I want to connect a few dots.

We are using the terms "walking by the Spirit" and "living by faith" interchangeably. This is important to remember! True righteousness will only be experienced if we learn to live by faith. Living by faith isn't quitting your job and hoping God pays your bills... though if he truly calls you to leave your job he will certainly provide for you!

Living by faith is maintaining the perspective that your old man, your sins, your sinful habits, and everything you inherited from Adam are dead once and for all through the person and work of our Messiah, Jesus Christ. Living by faith is also being willing to embrace the divine nature, to explore what it means to be born of God, and to take steps Jesus would take. That's the purpose of any good seed—to be transformed into the life-giving creation that it is. For the believer, this looks like growing up into Christlikeness! Though your righteousness may be in seed form, in due time you will see evidence that Christ has in fact come to dwell on the inside of you!

When we learn to walk by the Spirit we will actually be living by faith. And when we live by faith we will truly start experiencing what it means to be a new creation, partakers of the divine nature, the joy of being born of God, and having become the righteousness of God in Christ!

a HEALTHY SPIRITUAL ENVIRONMENT

THE BEAUTIFUL THING about discovering God's design for us is that it works!

Everything God does is beautiful! And growing up into salvation, maturing into Christlikeness, though filled with very real struggles, does not have to be a burden or a chore. The danger of trying to live our Christian lives without understanding God's design is that we end up trying to do spiritual things in our strength. This is man's design, and it doesn't work. The result of man's design? Exhaustion, burnout, and frustration. The result of God's design? Peace, rest, and contentment. It is God's perfect design alone that works. The very design that causes us to grow up into all Christ has purposed for us.

Everything God created grows in almost the exact same way. You start with a good seed (remember, that's you now!). Add in a healthy environment, nourishment, and time. When all of these are in place, God's amazing design is activated and we see growth! As we covered in the last chapter, through the death, burial, and resurrection of Jesus, you have become a good, righteous seed in Christ. Though much of what God has for you is currently still in seed form, when your life is planted in healthy soil and receives its nourishment, in time you will see powerful evidence that you are indeed *in Christ!* Just wait, growth is coming for you. And it's going to be magnificent.

So what is the fertile soil your life needs to be planted in so it flourishes with an everlasting growth that is from God?

The healthy environment for the born-again believer is *the new covenant*.

That's the soil. That's where you're going to take root. So what is this soil like? What is it not like? What makes it fertile? What makes it good?

The new covenant is your relational connection to God, the Father, made possible by the work of Jesus, and empowered by the Holy Spirit. This relationship with God is so wide, deep, high, and beautiful that it can be likened to an environment or an atmosphere. Our God is not only the soil in whom we are planted, but he is also the air we breathe, the water we drink, the sun we bask in, and the nutrients we need to grow. It may seem redundant to say the healthy environment we need to grow in is...God. But it is true and worth repeating over and over. There are distinct ways we can relate to and interact with God, but the basic, foundational principle is this...**without God we cannot grow up into him!**

Back we go to our seed analogy. Consider with me what an actual seed needs to grow. We can identify at least four key elements. The first is fertile (1) **soil** that is filled with the very nutrients the seed needs in order to transform into the fruit-yielding plant it is. Once the seedling sprouts through the ground, it begins converting (2) **sunlight** into energy through a process called photosynthesis. We've all heard this word many times in science classes but let's for a moment stare at this process and give it the wonder it deserves. The plant is *designed* to take the sun's energy and convert it into food it can then digest. This conversion allows the plant to grow. Wow. Are you amazed? I am. This process of photosynthesis is an important principle in God's design we will look at in more detail later. The final two necessary elements are (3) **water** and (4) **oxygen**.

How about we take a closer look at these elements? Within them holds the key to our own spiritual growth with God. Here we go!

1. THE SOIL

In continuing with our metaphor, the soil for the believer represents two aspects of the Christian life. First, it represents *our death, burial, and resurrection with Christ.*

Jesus said, "Truly, truly, I say to you, unless a grain of wheat falls into the earth and dies, it remains alone; but if it dies, it bears much fruit" (John 12:24, ESV). The Christian life starts with our death but results in much fruit! But before we can get to the fruit-bearing, we must fully appreciate a seed's beginning.

Before it ever bursts through the soil, a seed must first be planted into the ground, be transformed into a seedling, and become something wholly new. If we're honest, soil can seem scary if you don't understand God's design. We get easily fearful of God asking us, for a time, to be buried underneath the surface. Under the surface you are unseen, unrecognizable, and unable to do much other than to trust. This is an important process, and it shouldn't be rushed. Do not be surprised if, at the beginning of your journey with God, he hides you for a season. God is not trying to bury you! He is planting you so you can become the new creature you are destined to become in His son.

The second aspect of the soil represents *spiritual community*. God wants your life to be planted among other believers in Jesus so your roots comingle and connect with each other. Though it is almost always messy and challenging, the work required to stay connected to other believers is significantly less than the stress and burden of trying to live your Christian life alone.

Many new believers struggle to connect to a local church or a healthy spiritual family because they've experienced spiritual abuse, rejection, control, or some other pain that was never in the heart of God. This is tragic because when someone is hurt by those who claim to represent God, it creates an entrenched mindset in those who are afflicted. People wrongly assign God responsibility for the hurt.

If that is you, as a pastor and shepherd in the church, I want to say I am sorry for the pain you've experienced, and I want to ask for your forgiveness. God is not the author of control, manipulation, abuse, or perversion. His heart breaks over what you've experienced, and I believe he wants to redeem everything the enemy has tried to take away from you. Keep in mind that while there is no such thing as a perfectly healthy church, there are churches and spiritual communities much healthier than others. If you ask God, he will lead you to one. It is his design that you are connected, regularly, in a spiritual family where you can walk out all of the "one anothers" the Bible talks about in the New Testament.

2. SUNLIGHT

The second aspect needed for the seed is sunlight. I believe the powerful, radiant, life-giving sun is a picture of God's own powerful, radiant, life-giving son. It says in Revelation that the lamp or the light of heaven does not come from the sun or the moon, but from the Lamb of God, Jesus Christ himself (Revelation 21:23)!

So how do we receive the light of Jesus? There are rays of light, of love, and affection that flow from Jesus toward his children all of the time. One of the most powerful things we can do in our Christian life is to simply allow God to love us.

Picture your new life in Christ as a seedling, just peeking through the soil and beholding the heavens for the first time! The seedling is not required *to do* a bunch of things to grow. It simply needs to stay where it has been planted and allow the sun to shine upon it. Practically, I think this looks like setting aside time to simply wait on God and allow him to love you. God has announced his steadfast, never-ending love toward us by giving us His son Jesus. This love did not cease when Jesus died on a cross or rose from the grave. The same intensity and passion with which God loved us on the cross, He loves us with today!

Many of us fail to grow up into salvation because we do not trust in God's design. **One of the primary ways God grows his children in the new covenant is by simply bestowing His love upon them.** Busyness and distraction then become a sort of fleshly shade that hinders us from receiving the love of God. When we properly receive God's love, a spiritual photosynthesis occurs. The nature of God (the love and affection that comes to us like sunlight) hits our heart (by faith, we must *allow*

"One of the most powerful things we can do in our Christian life is to simply allow God to love us."

God to love us). This connection causes the *grace of God* to be poured out over us. And the grace of God is the spiritual nourishment that causes us to grow up into salvation so we look more and more like Jesus.

3. WATER

In the Bible the Holy Spirit is oftentimes likened to water. As it is with each of the elements, if you omit one element, God's design doesn't work. If you have a good seed, in fertile soil, receiving sunshine, but you don't give it water, it won't grow! The beautiful thing about God's design for growing things is that he has set in place governing principles that cannot and will not change. What does this mean for you? It means that once you *understand how* his design works, you will certainly see spiritual growth and transformation!

"If anyone is thirsty, let him come to Me and drink. He who believes in Me, as the Scripture said, 'From his innermost being will flow rivers of living water.' But this He spoke of the Spirit, whom those who believed in Him were to receive; for the Spirit was not yet given, because Jesus was not yet glorified." (John 7:37-39, NASB1995).

"For I will pour out water on the thirsty land And streams on the dry ground; I will pour out My Spirit on your offspring And My blessing on your descendants." (Isaiah 44:3, NASB1995)

"For by one Spirit we were all baptized into one body, whether Jews or Greeks, whether slaves or free, and we were all made to drink of one Spirit." (*1 Corinthians 12:13, NASB 1995*)

In the new covenant (the healthy environment) the water is the Holy Spirit. The Holy Spirit is not an impersonal force or a token of God's power. He is God the Spirit and the one *through* whom we experience the new covenant. We cannot know God, understand his Word, pray, share our faith, or do any other Christian thing without the Holy Spirit.

Jesus said of the Holy Spirit, "Nevertheless, I tell you the truth: it is to your advantage that I go away, for if I do not go away, the Helper will not come to you. But if I go, I will send him to you" (John 16:7, ESV). Jesus said it is to *our advantage* if he leaves and then sends the Spirit to us!

You do not have to live your life as a new believer in a dry wilderness! It is God's great delight that you never get so thirsty that you feel as though you are in a desert. **Too many believers claim to be in a wilderness season when God has given them access to rivers of living water in their innermost being.** So how do we receive this life-giving flow of God's own Spirit?

Through two steps: asking God for the Holy Spirit, and waiting with expectancy. That's it! Luke's gospel records, "If you then, who are evil, know how to give good gifts to your children, **how much more will the** heavenly Father give the Holy Spirit to those who ask him!" (Luke 11:13, ESV). How simple and straightforward is that? No hoops to jump through, no laundry list of to-dos...just *ask*. The Holy Spirit (water) is a gift and can never be earned. You cannot earn God's Spirit, his presence, or this wonderful river! It is simply a gift that comes to us as a result of Jesus' life and obedience as our Savior! The only requirement for us to receive the Spirit and to have confidence that the Father will actually give the Holy Spirit is being born again! You can pray something simple like this throughout your day, "Father, I ask you for the Holy Spirit!"

Now let's discuss step two, waiting with expectancy. There is an old saying, "If you pray for rain, don't forget to bring an umbrella." If you ask the Father for the Holy Spirit, don't forget to eagerly wait for and expect to receive him! Practically, I think this looks like setting aside time to receive from God. Some may ask, "How do I know I've received the Holy Spirit?" This is a great question. The Holy Spirit is a person and just like any person, he makes you feel a certain way. There are some people who, when you're around them, make you feel at peace. Others make you feel encouraged. Some people can make you feel afraid or downtrodden.

Here's what the person of the Holy Spirit will bring you: peace, confidence with God, and joy. He will encourage you, comfort you, and help you! So as you wait expectantly, knowing that the Father will fill you again and again with His Spirit, look for his peace, comfort, joy, and confidence.

4. OXYGEN

Take a deep breath with me. A really deep breath. Feel your ribcage rise and fall. Feel fresh, life-giving oxygen pouring into your body. Breathing happens from our hindbrain, we do it without thinking. But there is something particularly amazing when you stop, focus and breathe with intention. If you fail to give yourself oxygen, you will gasp for breath and eventually die. So it is with a little seedling. We've established that you're a good seed (righteous), planted in a healthy spiritual environment, with sunlight and water. But even if those three things were in place and you failed to give the seedling oxygen, it would rot and die. In order for the seedling to thrive, in addition to these other elements, it needs oxygen. Oxygen is **the grace of God.**

The grace of God is what you breathe in each moment of the day. It's what brings life, activation, and capacity to our lives. From a physical standpoint, oxygen keeps our brain transmitting, our blood pumping, and our organs functioning. Without it, we suffer. We gasp for air. We break down. So it is with the grace of God. Without it, we suffer, we gasp for air, and we break down. God's grace provides the believer with a sense of freedom, abundance, joy, and life-giving breath! You cannot grow up into salvation without the grace of God!

To understand the grace of God, which defines the new covenant relationship we now enjoy with God, we must briefly look at the old covenant that was in place *before* Jesus. The old covenant relationship God made with his people Israel was governed by a set of laws and commandments. You may have heard of the Ten Commandments? In order for Israel to remain in right standing with God (meaning in order for them to *be righteous)* they had to perform all of the Ten Commandments. Their connection and proximity to God hinged upon their obedience to the commandments. If they disobeyed, they were counted unrighteous and usually received some form of discipline, often being handed over to their enemies. If they repented, turned to God, and started walking in his commandments again, God would help his people and restore them again to peace and blessing.

The good news of the Gospel is that in Christ Jesus, this cycle of roller-coaster connection with God based on our own obedience has been broken!

The moment you surrendered your life to Jesus and were baptized into his death, burial, and resurrection, you were born into the new covenant! **The strength of this covenant, your relational connection with God, now rests upon the work of Christ instead of your own obedience.** Can you feel the freedom of that truth giving life to your mind, body, and spirit? Read it again with me. **Your relational connection with God now rests upon the work of Christ instead of your own obedience!** Talk about a flood of oxygen to the brain!

Now, make no mistake about it, our obedience within the new covenant is extremely important! But in the new covenant, our obedience does not come from our own strength, willpower, or desire. It is called *the obedience of faith*. This means that our ability to obey all of the commandments and instructions of the new covenant comes through a strong faith in the person and work of Jesus Christ. It is not a faith in the power of ourselves to do more, work harder, or be better. Our righteousness comes through one thing and one thing alone: the work, life, death, and resurrection of Jesus. That is the purpose of this book—to strengthen and establish you in the *faith* so that you can access the abundance of God's grace, the free gift of righteousness, and the indescribable joy of bearing Christlike fruit!

So how do we access this life-giving oxygen of the Spirit, the grace of God? We must fully and wholeheartedly rely upon the person and work of Jesus Christ to bring us close to God, our Father, and to help us in our time of need. As a new believer (or even if you've been walking with God a while and never knew this), you may continue to struggle with certain sinful thoughts or habits. The temptation is to believe that God is mad or frustrated with you. If you believe this, you may be tempted to try and regain a sense of closeness with God by doing a variety of spiritual things like going to church, reading your Bible, or confessing your sin. Though these things are important and good things to do, we cannot *rely upon them to make us feel righteous before God.*

We go to church, read our Bible, and confess our sin *within the new covenant* as children of God who are deeply loved by our Father. If you are struggling with sin you must defy every temptation to try with your own power and might to regain relational connection with God. The connection is already there because it flows from Jesus' work, not ours. This is what the Bible calls the *good fight of faith*, resisting temptation to trust and rely upon anything or anyone except Jesus Christ and his steadfast love towards us.

In order to experience this life-giving breath of God, the glorious oxygen of the new covenant called grace, we must focus all of our energy and effort on keeping our attention on Jesus. How amazingly simple is that? There isn't a long to-do list in the new covenant Kingdom of God. There's one to-do: keep your attention on Jesus. Reading the Scriptures, praying and fasting, and going to church are wonderful activities for us to do that will help keep our attention on Jesus.

The result of our eyes and ears being fixed on Jesus is that he (Jesus) will continue to author and perfect our faith in him (Hebrews 12:2). This means the more we look at Jesus, the more our faith grows and gets firmly rooted in him. This also means that *the only way to experience the life-giving oxygen of grace is by faith.* The Bible says, "For by grace you have been saved through faith. And this is not your own doing; it is the gift of God, not a result of works, so that no one may boast" (Ephesians 2:8-9, ESV).

This is perhaps one of the most important lessons for born-again believers. The same way you were saved (born again) is the same way you are going to grow up into salvation. *By grace, through faith.* The reason for this is that God doesn't want us to boast in our own righteousness or piety. If you see someone who looks like Jesus, meaning they walk in righteousness, holiness, purity, power, and love, it is because they have learned to walk by grace through faith. They did not earn or discipline themselves into a life of holiness. As you learn to trust in God's perfect design, you will discover that he is able to deliver you from sinful thoughts and habits. He is also able to form and fashion you into the image of Christ. This is all by the free gift of righteousness and the abundance of grace!

> "...by grace through faith."

The new covenant is the perfect environment for you, a brand-new righteous son or daughter of Christ, to grow up into salvation! Simply allow your life to be planted in the **soil**, a spiritual community, be baptized (if you haven't already!), and identify with the death, burial, and resurrection of Jesus. Spend time basking in the **sunlight** of God's affection and love for you! Ask the Father for the **water** of God's Spirit, and give him time to water your life! Finally, breathe deep of his grace, the glorious **oxygen** of the new covenant!

As you do this, you will notice that sinful thoughts and behaviors will begin to wither up and die. You will discover the beauty of Jesus being formed in your thoughts, desires, and even actions! Your life will take on new meaning and purpose. The old ways of existing will be replaced by new ways of thriving. Prayer will become like breathing. Reading the Scriptures will become like feasting on warm bread that has just come out of the oven. Your spiritual community will be like iron that sharpens you into a man or woman of God. Your new covenant environment will become a source of covering and shade during seasons of trials and suffering. The fellowship of the Holy Spirit will be like water to your thirsty soul! What a wonderful vision of salvation and growth that we have been invited into with our God!

CHAPTER 3

SPIRITUAL NOURISHMENT

AS MY DEAR friend, Michael Miller, always says, "Seeds have needs." The beauty of God's design is that he creates seeds with needs. If you meet the needs of the seeds, the design is activated and growth ensues. This is ultimately my desire and the purpose of this book, to help you understand how things grow. To help you understand how *you* grow. If you understand it, you can apply it to your life and ultimately help others discover and apply it as well.

As we've discussed previously, a healthy seed needs a good environment. Part of that healthy environment is the **nourishment** the seed receives. In this chapter we will more closely examine four unique ways we are nourished within the new covenant. What I love about the word "nourish" is that it speaks to something happening to us. We don't necessarily nourish ourselves.

A mother nourishes a baby with her milk. A gardener nourishes his own garden by watering it and making sure the soil has what it needs for the plant to grow. So too will your God nourish you! Let's look at four ways we are nourished in the new covenant!

When you're diving into a topic, there's no better place to begin than the beginning...the definition of a word.

> **Nourish** / 'nəriSH/ *verb* 1. *provide with the food or other substances necessary for growth, health, and good condition.* 2. *keep (a feeling or belief) in one's mind, typically for a long time.*

I love both of these definitions. The first speaks of a Provider who will supply you with the spiritual food and substances necessary for you to grow. This is the gift that keeps on giving! In the new covenant, growth always starts with receiving. How refreshing is that? And isn't it a bit counterintuitive for our human brain? We start by receiving, not by doing, striving, or accomplishing.

We receive the love of God, the nourishment of God, and then we respond. We respond with a thankful heart, with worship, with prayer, and with obedience! But God always initiates with us! Your confidence in your future growth should not and cannot hinge on your ability to obey God perfectly. Instead, it must be rooted in God's commitment and desire to nourish the seed of righteousness given to you! There are many ways we can partner with God's design to be nourished, but I want to highlight four specific verses that speak to our spiritual nourishment.

THE NOURISHING ROOT OF ISRAEL

If you are reading this and you are not Jewish, it is important for you to know that before the gospel ever came to you or to me, it first came to Abraham (Galatians 3:8). When God wanted to redeem the world back to himself, he started a family with a man named Abraham. Abraham received a miracle, a promised son named Isaac. Isaac and his wife gave birth to Jacob, who eventually, after wrestling with God, was renamed Israel, which means "fighter of God" or "triumphant with God." This man Israel became the father of twelve sons who would eventually become the twelve tribes of Israel. Through this family line God has

> "In the new covenant, growth always starts with receiving."

made some very great and fantastic promises, many of which are fulfilled and many are yet to be fulfilled!

So why do I bring up the nation (family) of Israel when talking about spiritual nourishment? Because if we are not Jewish, and we've been born again, we need to understand that we are being grafted into Israel's story. The beauty and promise of the Gospel is that both Jews and Gentiles (everyone who is *not Jewish*) would become *one new man* in Christ (Ephesians 2:14-

15). The promise of relational connection and intimacy with God was formerly only made available to the Jewish people. *But, through the work and person of Jesus Christ, **that same unity and relational connection is now available to the entire world, to all of us!*** Look at what the apostle Paul has to say about this in the context of us being nourished.

> *"But if some of the branches were broken off, and you, although a wild olive shoot, were grafted in among the others and now share in the **nourishing** root of the olive tree, do not be arrogant toward the branches. If you are, remember it is not you who support the root, but the root that supports you"* (Romans 11:17-18, ESV).

The picture here is of a native olive tree having wild olive shoots grafted into it. You and I (the Gentiles reading this) are likened to wild olive shoots. We are not native to the olive tree! This verse only makes sense if we have an understanding of grafting. Grafting is a common technique used to propagate fruit that is genetically the same as the original plant. To do this, a branch would be broken off the native tree and a wild olive shoot would be spliced into the native tree. The wild olive shoot would then become a part of the native olive tree, being nourished by the deep roots of the tree. The picture here is that we are being blessed, nourished, and strengthened by inheriting the spiritual promises of relational proximity to the Living God that was initially only given to the nation of Israel. God wants to propagate Christ in you and me by connecting us to his family! The encouragement to us then is not to be arrogant towards Israel and other believers. Your spiritual nourishment is not something you earn! We are instead grafted in by a master gardener. This beautiful metaphor is cause for thankfulness, humility, and generosity with the life that we now have in Christ.

CHRIST, OUR HUSBAND

"For no one ever hated his own flesh, but **nourishes** *and cherishes it, just as Christ does the church"* *(Ephesians 5:29, ESV).*

One of the most profound and mysterious truths of the new covenant is that we, the church, are now engaged to Jesus (Ephesians 5:32). We as the church are called his Bride throughout Scriptures. He has delivered us from the power of Satan, sin, and death, and he's coming back for us in a triumphant return. He has caused us to be born again and by his grace, the washing of his Spirit, one day we will marry Jesus as a pure and spotless Bride (2 Corinthians 11:2). This can be a confusing metaphor but it is an important one. The invitation for us as believers is to wrestle with the thought that God can actually make us as pure, righteous, and blameless as his son! It speaks of God's desire to be intimate with us. If we are honest, this is hard to grasp and that is okay! The point here is Jesus sees us as his own Bride. And as any faithful husband would do, he has promised to nourish you and me! But what does this nourishment look like? How does Jesus nourish us?

One of the primary ways Jesus nourishes us is by reminding us of who he is and what he has done for us. He strengthens us with his own nature. More specifically, he nourishes us with his love. Jesus preached a sermon in John 6 where he describes himself as the Bread of Life! He tells his followers that his flesh is food and his

> "As God's children, we have permission to look like him in how we think, feel, and act!"

blood is a life-giving drink (John 6:55)! He promised that those who learn to feed on his flesh and drink his blood will have eternal life (John 6:54)! What? Jesus was not advocating cannibalism. He's saying that the depth and strength of his love for humanity, revealed on the cross, would become a nourishing feast for his followers. Jesus nourishes us with bread and wine, his broken body and shed blood, as an ongoing reminder of his great love for us!

In reminding us of his love, he nourishes the seed of righteousness within us. The Bible says the Spirit bears witness that we are in fact children of God (Romans 8:16)! As God's children, we have permission to look like him in how we think, feel, and act! If Jesus is merciful, patient, and pure, then we too are invited to be merciful, patient, and pure. How? By trying to be merciful? No! By recognizing that the Merciful One has come to dwell inside of you. He nourishes our new nature by showing us what it looks like full-grown! Let me give you an example...

There was a time when my boys were younger that they often frustrated me by *being boys* at the wrong time. They would roughhouse, shout or wildly run around at seemingly all the wrong times. We'd be trying to clean up the house, get out the door, or wind down for the night, and there the boys would be, bouncing off the walls. In those moments, I would feel frustration and anger begin to well up inside of me, and more than once I tried to control their behavior by yelling at them or giving vent to my anger. I knew it was wrong because it didn't *feel* right and I *knew* that the anger of man never produces the righteousness of God (James 1:20). So I started asking God to give me patience. A few weeks later I was reading my Bible and came across this verse...

"Take my yoke upon you, and learn from me, for I am gentle and lowly in heart, and you will find rest for your souls" (Matthew 11:29, ESV).

The phrase, *"I am gentle"* leapt out at me. It was as if Jesus was whispering to me, "I am gentle." But even God's whisper is powerful! That phrase kept rattling around in my heart and mind. I didn't immediately connect it to the issue I was having with getting angry with my kids until one day I was faced with the familiar situation of my boys being disobedient. I could feel the frustration and anger rising within me yet again.

But all of a sudden I heard the whisper coming from a deeper place, "*I am gentle.*" In this whisper was an invitation to let the *Gentle One* manifest himself *through me* to my boys. Though I could still feel the frustration, the righteousness of Christ was stronger! I knelt down and gently invited my boys to come close. I calmly instructed them that what they were doing was out of place, and I reminded them of what we needed to do. I was amazed! I didn't need more patience! I just needed to let the Patient One out! Don't get distracted with what you don't have! Don't be discouraged with old thought patterns or sin habits.

You are a partaker of the divine nature, having been born of God, and Jesus will nourish you *out of the old life* and *into his image* by revealing his nature to you through His Word. As you spend time in God's Word, the Spirit will reveal Jesus to you! As Jesus is revealed to you, his likeness and character will come out of you!

TOGETHER, WE ARE NOURISHED

*"and not holding fast to the Head, from whom the whole body, **nourished** and knit together through its joints and ligaments, grows with a growth that is from God" (Colossians 2:19).*

Spiritual nourishment isn't just about what you get directly from God and his Word. One very important aspect of God's design for you and me to grow up into salvation is that we are meant to do it *together*. Paul is encouraging the church of Colossae not to get distracted by all the laws and special days but to simply hold fast to the Head (Jesus). As we hold fast to Jesus, the whole body will be nourished and knit together! God's nourishment will not only connect us to him, but also to one another! And through this divine connection with God and each other, we will grow with "God growth!" God's growth is faster and more exponential than just a natural growth! The growth that is from God means that we will start to look like Jesus in ways that no man can produce. Remember the wild olive shoot? Its natural growth can never match the growth it experiences once it is grafted into the tree. As we partner with God's design for spiritual growth, know it is his plan that we grow together!

With humanism running rampant in our nation, the temptation can be to apply these spiritual principles to our own lives at the neglect of living them out in a spiritual community. Proverbs says, "Whoever isolates himself seeks his own desire; he breaks out against all sound judgment" (Proverbs 18:1, ESV). If a beautiful, perfect seed is never planted in soil it will never grow! The world will tell you that you can grow all by yourself, but it is God's perfect design that we are connected with other believers. Though it may *feel* easier initially to try and grow by yourself, it is not sustainable.

The body of Christ is *one body* with many members.

You're a part of that body now. You are grafted in. And we as a church, if we want to walk in the fullness of what Christ paid for, are going to need to come together and stay together. Our connection to each other isn't based on our preferences, some style of worship music, or denomination. It is based on the fact that our life comes from the Head, Jesus! He is the source of our life!

Our common faith in Jesus is the only thing that has the power to bring us together. In this same breath, we must also remember that our growth is not just about us! The stronger our faith and the more mature we become, by the grace of God, the more accurately we as a church can represent Jesus to each other and to the world. One body. Many members. One mission.

TRUTHS OF THE FAITH

"If you point these things out to the brothers and sisters, you will be a good minister of Christ Jesus, **nourished** *on the truths of the faith and of the good teaching that you have followed"* (1 Timothy 4:6, NIV).

One of the ways we are nourished by God in the new covenant is through the teaching and preaching of the truths of the faith! Truth will nourish you! In fact, Jesus said that the truth would set us free (John 8:32)!

If you try to live the Christian life by how you feel or by the latest cultural conversation, you will never grow and you will never find freedom. Many Christians are being deceived because they have not been established and nourished on the *truths of the faith*. Instead, they are being led astray by cultural conversations and the ongoing banter of self-proclaimed gurus who have no knowledge of God. What are these truths of the faith? A better question is, *who is this truth?*

The truths of the faith will always point to Jesus, his nature, his work of salvation, and the appropriate response of faith to those who receive him. If you hear a message or teaching that does not reveal Jesus, point to Jesus, or cause you to want to know Jesus, be careful. There are lots of messengers preaching lots of things! But if the truth they are preaching doesn't lead you to Jesus, then they are not going the right Way!

Jesus is the Way, the Truth, and the Life! Jesus also said, "Sanctify them in the truth; your word is truth" (John 17:17, ESV). Paul says, "Of this you have heard before in the word of the truth, the gospel" (Colossians 1:5, ESV). The Word of truth is the Gospel! It is the continual revelation of Christ (Galatians 1:11) to us so that we can continue to live by faith, empowered and sanctified by God's grace!

Practically, you want to regularly be reminded of truth through Christ-centered preaching, teaching, and Bible study of who Jesus is, what he has done, and what it means for you. As Christians, we must actively pursue the truth, keep our eyes on the truth, and not be tempted by the world's way, which never produces life. This is how you continue in the faith and ensure the truths of the faith are nourishing you into Christlikeness.

Truth nourishes us into Christlikeness and it also nourishes us into peaceful living. If we take a look at our current culture, we see peace is a longing unfulfilled. People want peace, people search for peace, and people keep coming up empty. Why does it seem nearly impossible to find? We've been looking in the wrong places—career paths, travel destinations, self-help books, political associations, social groups, and on and on the list can go. Trying to find peace in the world is futile because there is only one source of peace: the truths of God. When we enjoy union with God and meditate on who he is and what he's done, peace will flood every part of our lives. It's a steadfast peace built on an unchanging, immovable God, and now, you get to enjoy it.

So we are nourished into Christlikeness and peace within the new covenant by *(1) Israel, (2) Jesus himself, as our Husband, (3) within spiritual community and by being connected and grafted into the spiritual inheritance, and (4) the truths of the faith.*

We've journeyed far together, haven't we? We've covered a lot of ground and unpacked this beautiful beginning of your faith. We have established that you are a good seed, you've been planted in the new covenant, and you will be constantly nourished by Christ himself...the only thing left to understand is the time required in order to see the growth we long for!

CHAPTER 4

TIME:
The GROWTH PROCESS

WHEN YOU UNDERSTAND God's design for growth, time becomes your friend. Imagine waking up every day in your spiritual journey filled with excitement and expectation that you're going to see good fruit! Imagine knowing each day is causing you to be transformed more and more into the image of Christ. Imagine feeling rest and peace about your future instead of fear or worry.

The power of understanding God's design for growth is that it gives us confidence we are in the right place at the right time! If we don't understand God's design for growth, we start to feel like time is against us, like time is the enemy. We wonder if the things we are doing are actually working. We start comparing our journey with someone else's, feeling dissatisfied with where we are in life, and experiencing confusion about what's next. But I have good news. God owns time. He authors it. And his desire for you is that you understand how to grow in his time and partner with his design.

How often have you heard someone say, "I'm just so busy right now!"? As the gift of technology has made our lives more efficient and seemingly given us more time, how is it that so many of us are actually busier than ever? Part of the problem is we've valued being productive over being fruitful. Being productive is all about eliminating inefficiency and maximizing the use of our time so we can produce more. Being fruitful is about tapping into God's design and fulfilling the unique purpose for which we were created. Productivity produces stress. Fruitfulness produces peace. Trying to be more productive requires you to sweat while being fruitful requires you to simply remain in God's design.

Do you remember the scene in The Lion King where Mufasa sits Simba down and tells him not to venture into the dark areas of the kingdom? Like Mufasa, I have a few "don't wander into the dark areas" warnings for you. Mufasa's warnings for Simba are for his good, as are mine for you.

If we stop partnering with God's design, time seems to become our enemy. We feel like we are constantly falling behind, never doing enough, and missing out on the perfect will of God. I'm surprised by how many Christians I meet who feel this way. There is a sense of purposelessness if you are not planted in the new covenant, grounded in the love of God, and enjoying a real experience of union with Christ. If we find ourselves in this place we begin to compare our lives with other people who are doing great things for God, and we are tempted to feel as though we should be doing more. Imagine a seedling comparing itself to a mature plant! Think of the tender little plant trying to do more so it can become like its mature counterpart. This type of thinking produces feelings of stress, anxiety, and frustration. We try to do more but after nonstop effort and sweating around the clock, we look up to discover we haven't made any true progress. We see the same sin habits or earthly tendencies. We wonder why what we've done hasn't translated into changed behavior or feelings. It is because when we rely on what we do to change us, we are inadvertently cutting ourselves off from God's grace, his nourishing change agent in our lives. The doing and the work of the Christian life flow from our connection to God and our awareness of his empowering presence. The Bible says it this way,

> "Being fruitful is about tapping into God's design and fulfilling the unique purpose for which we were created."

"For we are his workmanship, created in Christ Jesus for good works, which God prepared beforehand, that we should walk in them" (Ephesians 2:10, ESV).

The word for workmanship comes from the Greek word poiéma, which is where we get the word "poem." It literally means "a thing made." The picture here is that you and I have now been created, a thing made and designed by God to do good, Christlike works. These things we do will be a function and byproduct of our new identity in Christ.

Picture it like this. If you go to an apple orchard and study a row of apple trees, you might find some of the apple trees are laden with fruit and some of the trees are not bearing any fruit at all. The purpose of an apple tree is to make apples. So we could say of the apple trees that are actually bearing fruit, those trees are working! They are functioning (working) according to their design. When they are bearing fruit, we can assume a good seed was planted in a healthy environment, it has been nourished according to design, and the appropriate amount of time has elapsed for it to grow and bear fruit.

In the same manner, we can look at the trees not bearing fruit and jump to a variety of conclusions. No fruit must mean a bad seed. Or a bad environment. Or a lack of nourishment. But these conclusions miss one key component: time. Perhaps the tree is simply not mature enough to start bearing fruit. Did you know it takes a healthy, standard-sized apple tree up to eight years to actually bear fruit? Healthy seed, good environment, plenty of nourishment, the right timing.

You walk along the orchard a bit further and come

to another tree. Its leaves look dry and the soil around the base is cracked and hard. The reason this apple tree might not be bearing fruit is that it's not being nourished properly. Perhaps the soil doesn't have all the tree needs for the fruit to actually be formed. Or maybe the tree isn't getting enough sunlight. All of these things can represent spiritual truths that will help us understand the valuable role time has in our spiritual growth.

In the case of the healthy apple tree, we can see the work of the tree is simply bearing fruit in its specified time. This is a picture of your life being established as a good seed, planted in a healthy environment, and well-nourished over many years. You will bear fruit. You are designed for it, planted for it, pruned for it, and nourished for it. Certainly there are years that are harder for the tree to survive than others. Perhaps a severe drought makes it difficult to hydrate the branches and the leaves. Maybe extreme winter tests the roots of the tree. The changes in seasons and the picture of this tree remaining planted in the same place, day after day and year after year, is a spiritual reality for us. It represents a life of faith, established in the truths of the Gospel, and unmoved by the difficulties and challenges we all face.

In your Christian life you will face different seasons and many trials. It will sometimes feel like nothing is happening. Other times it will feel like everything is happening to you. You won't always discern or feel in the moment that you are growing or being nourished. The challenge for you will be not questioning whether or not you're a good seed, not questioning the healthy environment (even though a harsh winter may not feel healthy, it's normal!), and not resisting God's nourishing affection through it all. The confidence we have is that no matter what comes our way, our life is now hidden with Christ in God (Colossians 3:3). This means that regardless of how hard the season or how long our transformation and growth process takes, we know we will overcome because our life has now been joined to the Lord.

Understanding that time is a critical component for any living thing to grow will produce patience for ourselves and for those around us. Can you imagine getting impatient with an apple tree for not bearing apples after only a year? Once the owner of the orchard told you it takes a minimum of eight years for an apple tree to mature and start bearing fruit, you would know to tend to the tree without expecting immediate fruit. We must do the same with ourselves. Our spiritual journey is not dissimilar to an apple tree growing.

Though we cannot place an exact time frame on our progress and growth, we can rest assured that true transformation takes place in time. This is not to be confused with the supernatural power and grace of God to save, deliver, and heal us in a moment. This speaks of the process of spiritual maturity whereby we find freedom from sin, greater intimacy with our Father, and the power to walk like Christ.

Spiritual maturity does not happen with one encounter. Nothing in God's created order grows or matures that way. Life-changing encounters with God are to be expected and desired but those moments are unto lasting growth and transformation. So how do you know, now that you're born again, if time is working for you or against you?

- Are you holding fast to the amazing truth you have been born again? Are you continuing to marvel that God, through Jesus Christ, has forgiven your sins and caused you to be born again? Are you still amazed you are a new creation and your life is now hidden with Christ? If yes, move onto the next question. If not, you must revisit this truth and thank God for it! Allow his peace to wash over you once again, knowing you are forgiven and he has given you the gift of righteousness.

- Are you actively engaged and planted in the healthy environment that is the new covenant? Are you in the good soil of a local church family? If you're in a season of hiddenness under the soil, are you fighting it or embracing it? Are you content with knowing God sees and loves you? Are you setting aside time to receive the affections and warmth of Jesus' love towards you? Are you asking God for the Holy Spirit? Are you breathing in the oxygen of his grace? If yes, move onto the next question.

- Are you being nourished by Jesus and his Word? Are you receiving his love towards you as demonstrated through his broken body and shed blood (John 6)?

As you continue in these precious truths of the faith, you can rest in God's design that you are indeed moving towards greater freedom, deeper intimacy with God, and a transformed life. If you can't answer yes to these questions, then I encourage you to go back to them and spend some time with God and with your spiritual community engaging with these truths. Acknowledge where you've been distracted or lost sight of God's design. Ask God for grace and strength to keep your eyes on Jesus and the truth about who He is. Ask him to nourish you with his smile and to wash you with his Spirit.

In the new covenant, time is now your friend. Each day is a gift of God filled with surprises of new growth, longings fulfilled, and joy.

CHAPTER 5

YOUR PURPOSE
in LIFE

AS HUMANS, WE long for meaning. Meaning in our lives, meaning in our relationships, meaning in our day-to-day and our year-to-year. People search with great effort and time, often coming up empty.

I have good news for you! Your search is over. The very moment you said yes to God's invitation, you were given meaning, purpose, and direction.

Identifying and explaining our purpose as Christians is the goal of this final chapter. Read it with your new eyes, from the vantage point of a righteous seed firmly planted in good, nourishing soil.

How do you know you are growing up into salvation? How do you know you are partnering with God's design? What is your purpose in life now that you are born again?

These are really important questions we should ask

ourselves as we walk out our Christian journey. If you do not know what "growth" looks like as a Christian, it will be easy to get discouraged. If you are not confident you are walking in the Spirit and according to God's design, you will start "troubleshooting" your life, trying to figure out what is wrong. This might seem innocent enough, but it can result in a lot of grief and wasted time. If you don't know you're already in the right place, you will most certainly spin your wheels searching for some other place.

Many believers think the *right place* has to do with what church they attend or what job they have, and though these things are important, they are not the most important thing. The truth is, the *right* place in the Christian life is *in* Christ. This is a spiritual reality you can experience, no matter what your job is, where you live, what church you attend, or what your finances are like. When you were born again, God placed Christ *in you* (by the Holy Spirit) and he put you *in Christ* (by the Holy Spirit). Jesus explains to us in John 15 when he says, "Abide in me, and I in you." And again, "Whoever abides in me and I in him, he it is that bears much fruit, for apart from me you can do nothing" (John 15:4-5, ESV).

> "The truth is, the *right* place in the Christian life is *in* Christ."

Did you see your place and purpose? In one sentence, Jesus gave us the end goal of the Christian life. He has defined success: to be in Christ and to bear fruit.

When you are in the right place, you *will* fulfill your purpose of bearing fruit. That is a promise to us. Jesus goes on to say, "By this my Father is glorified, that you bear much fruit and so prove to be my disciples. As the Father has loved me, so have I loved you. Abide in my love" (John 15:8-9, ESV). The proof you belong to Jesus and you've been born again is that you are bearing much fruit! And a life of fruitfulness is what brings glory to your Father in heaven! It makes him so proud to see you bearing fruit!

YOUR CALLING

It's simple, isn't it? Your purpose and high calling in life are to simply belong to Jesus, to abide in His love, and to allow his beautiful character and nature to be formed inside of you. As he forms his character inside of you (we call this the fruit of the Holy Spirit) he will begin to empower you to walk like Christ.

Remember our jalapeño plant from chapter 1? If a jalapeño plant is designed to bear jalapeños and an apple tree is made by God to bear apples, what fruit is a Christian meant to bear?

The answer? Christlikeness. When we belong to God, we start to bear fruit that resembles Jesus himself. Our hearts are molded into his and therefore our behavior and lifestyle are molded into his. Simply put: our old self dies, and our new righteous seed begins to grow.

To become like Christ and to reveal what he is really like is your high calling! Now this calling is deep and wide and is experienced in a number of ways. If we try to accomplish this in our own strength, it *is* impossible. But if we partner with God's design, we will be transformed into his image—not by human effort or striving—but by holy, Spirit-filled growth and change!

Now that you are born again, your first and primary calling is to learn to belong to Christ.

Paul wrote to the Romans, "including you who are called to belong to Jesus Christ" (Romans 1:6, ESV). Their calling was to simply belong. Belonging to Christ can be compared with the invitation in John 15 to abide in Christ. Simply put, it means to stay where God put you! And where did he put you? In Christ. To belong to Christ means to keep your heart soft and appreciative toward the magnificent truth that we have been joined to Christ by grace, through faith, and experienced by His Spirit.

To belong to Christ speaks of learning to connect with God in your heart through thanksgiving, worship, prayer, time in his Word, and meditating upon him. If you do not place a value on learning what it means to belong to Christ, you will get busy doing many things *for God* instead of many things *with God*. Doing things *for God* almost always results in peace and joy decreasing and burnout increasing. In the same way, doing things *with God* instead of *for him* results in lasting joy, perseverance through seasons, and a peace only found in union with God. You were made to belong.

BECOME A RECEIVER

The Bible says we love because he first loved us (1 John 4:19). To belong to God is to first accept your new reality: you have been born again, forgiven of your sins, made new in Christ, received grace and righteousness, and you now have the right to become his child (John 1:12-13). The ones who embrace this calling to belong to Christ are the ones who continually practice receiving free gifts from God. Before we can ever give anything to God or do anything in his name, we must first simply receive.

Practically speaking, when you spend time with God, start with remembrance. Who has God been to you? Remember the peace and joy of having all of your sins forgiven! Remember his work on the cross and his resurrection. Enjoy the truth that your life is now hidden with Christ (Colossians 3:3). Let God speak his words of affirmation and love over you. Directly from the Bible, here are just a few of his words toward you as His child:

- "You did not choose me, but I chose you and appointed you so that you might go and bear fruit—fruit that will last—and so that whatever you ask in my name the Father will give you" (John 15:16, NIV).
- "But you are a chosen people, a royal priesthood, a holy nation, God's special possession,

that you may declare the praises of him who called you out of darkness into his wonderful light" (1 Peter 2:9, NIV).

- "For we are God's handiwork, created in Christ Jesus to do good works, which God prepared in advance for us to do" (Ephesians 2:10, NIV).
- "Therefore, if anyone is in Christ, he is a new creation; old things have passed away; behold, all things have become new" (2 Corinthians 5:17, NKJV).
- "Now you are the body of Christ and individually members of it" (1 Corinthians 12:27, ESV).
- "See what kind of love the Father has given to us, that we should be called children of God; and so we are. The reason why the world does not know us is that it did not know him" (1 John 3:1, ESV).
- "For you have died, and your life is hidden with Christ in God" (Colossians 3:3, ESV).
- "But now in Christ Jesus you who once were far off have been brought near by the blood of Christ" (Ephesians 2:13, NIV).

For me, the above list is like water for my soul, a constant reminder of God's love and affection toward me. Don't resist his kindness, his mercy, and his patience. Believe it or not, one of the most common struggles believers have is actually believing the love God has for them! This is why we must daily choose to live in the new covenant. If you find you are tired, burned out, or frustrated in your walk with God, it is likely you have wandered away from first love. First love is the beautiful truth that He loved us first! And he always loves us first! Our life is simply a response to his extravagant love.

How do I know I'm receiving from God? What Christlike fruit should I look for?

The promise is this: if you abide in him and he in you, you will bear much fruit! There are two types of spiritual fruit: internal fruit, which is the fruit of the Spirit; and external fruit, which are the works and ministry of

> "Our life is simply a response to his extravagant love."

Jesus. Though these fruits are inseparable from each other, it is good to recognize the difference between them.

INTERNAL FRUIT: FRUIT OF THE SPIRIT

One of the first signs of spiritual growth in your life will be the fruit of the Spirit.

> *"But the fruit of the Spirit is love, joy, peace, patience, kindness, goodness, faithfulness, gentleness, self-control;* **against such things there is no law**" *(Galatians 5:22-23, ESV, emphasis added).*

You can't make this fruit happen. You can't work

harder, work faster, or work better to experience the fruit of the Spirit. The fruit of the Spirit is just that—the Spirit's work in you. This isn't fruit you tape on your tree externally; it's fruit you allow to be grown from the inside out. There is no law against it, meaning it is not subject to man's efforts. You can't demand this fruit to grow in your life. It is fruit. It is a byproduct and work of the Spirit in your life. When you surrender and yield to the Holy Spirit, you will discover the fruit of the Spirit growing beautifully, wildly in you.

When you start walking by faith within God's design, he will do an exchange in your heart. He replaces selfishness, sadness, anxiety, impatience, faithlessness, harshness, and a lack of self-control for His fruit, the fruit of the Spirit. You will notice negative internal thought patterns and feelings wither away as God causes fruit like love, joy, and peace to come forth. This is a sign you are growing! You will discover what previously caused you anger and jealousy no longer has the same power. You will find where it was once hard to receive and give love, it now flows more freely. You will see where anxiety once sat on a throne in your mind, it is now replaced by the Prince of Peace.

For most of us, our physical circumstances do not immediately change when we are born again. It is your inner life that shifts and transforms. Your thoughts and emotions will begin to align with Jesus and the atmosphere of heaven. Though these things do not happen all at once, trust that they will happen! And the joy it will bring you when you discover he is in fact transforming you from the inside out will be hard to contain! And you shouldn't try to contain it. It is intended to grow and flow, and it is our calling to let it. This brings us to an important part of your new life in Christ.

GOD IS DOING SO MUCH: WHAT DO WE DO?

It is natural to want to know what you should do! So much of this book is about renewing your mind to the truth of God's design and the power of the new covenant. But as you enjoy life in the new covenant and you see and experience the person and work of Christ, there is an appropriate response and action we can take as believers!

The most appropriate response to the Gospel, to Christ, and his life-giving Spirit at work in and through us is *thanksgiving, praise, and worship*. We thank God for what he's done! We praise him for what he's like! We worship him because we are in love with him!

One of the most common ways (not the only way!) we thank, praise, and worship him is through corporate worship and prayer services. When you go to church or a corporate prayer and worship service, you are going, not primarily to receive something *new* but to give thanks and honor God for what he has already done! Of course, God will meet with you, speak with you, and fulfill your needs, but it is important we remember who he is and what he has already done! If he didn't do anything else, we could still praise him forever! We could give thanks for eternity for all of his works! We would never get tired of worshiping him because of his beauty and his majesty.

In addition to gathering with our spiritual family to praise and worship, we are also called to live lives of thanksgiving, praise, and worship. This looks like, "And whatever you do, in word or deed, do everything in the name of the Lord Jesus, giving thanks to God the Father through him" (Colossians 3:17, ESV).

Did you see that? *Whatever you do!* You can do the dishes, go on a run, work your job, change diapers, or go to dinner with a friend—all in the name of the Lord! This means you are mindful and aware of God's grace, his kindness, and his goodness that has afforded you the opportunity to live your life! It is to live a life of thankfulness! It is to live a life of praise! I like to practice this by finding reasons throughout my day to be grateful! When I'm making my bed in the mornings, I might say, "Thank you, God, for a warm bed to sleep in." If I'm picking up toys my kids have left around the house, I might pray something like, "Thank you, God, for the gift of children, for the blessing of all these toys!" Living a life of gratitude, praise, joy, and peace is one of the greatest ways to share your faith with those around you.

EXTERNAL FRUIT: THE WORKS OF JESUS

The Christian life is not merely an inner reality. As beautiful as the inner life in Christ is, it must certainly change and transform (*in his time!*) the way we speak and act. God has called us to holiness, to righteous living, to a life of serving out of love, and to extravagantly bless and give to others what He has given to us. This too is fruit that comes through abiding in the love of God. As we grow in our awareness of God's love and his abiding presence, we will be empowered to walk just like Jesus.

John says emphatically, "By this we know that we are in him: whoever says he abides in him ought to walk in the same way in which he walked" (1 John 2:5-6, ESV).

If we are going to be a Jesus people who abide, we must also be a Jesus people who walk in the same way in which he walked! And how did he walk?

- He walked in utter dependence on his Father (John 5:30).
- He walked in grace and truth (John 1:17).
- He walked in power over sin, sickness, and the devil (the New Testament).
- He walked in signs and wonders, promising we would do more! (John 14:12).
- He walked in forgiveness in the face of injustice (Luke 23:34).

- He walked in love, laying his life down (John 15:13).
- He walked in humility and servanthood (Matthew 11:29, Matthew 23:11).

There are full books that have been written about the life of Christ! Though we don't have time in this book to fully explain and describe what it means to *walk like Christ*, this short list has been compiled here for further study. If you have been born again, you will find deep within you a longing to experience all of the things listed above. You were made for this life! You were born again, in his image, to grow up and mature into his likeness! Don't be discouraged or lose heart because you don't see these things right away! Trust in God. Trust in your Father who has loved you with an everlasting love! This high calling and purpose of manifesting the life of Christ is never something you can earn by your own piety or religious efforts! He doesn't want us to boast about our own strength! It is by the grace of God, through faith, that we are to grow up on the inside *and* grow up on the outside.

TIME TO GROW

You are born again and have been introduced to his wonderful plan for your life. What can you do to ensure you grow up into salvation and enjoy the journey along the way?

Remember the five simple elements we have covered.

- You're a good seed.
- You've been planted in the new covenant, into a spiritual family.
- God will nourish you.
- Time is your friend.
- You will fulfill God's purpose for your life.

Remember that everything grows in the same way. It doesn't mean everything grows at the same time or with the same speed! Perhaps the most important thing you can remember is it was God that initiated a relationship with you! Hopefully by now you understand your spiritual growth and momentum doesn't begin and end with you! You are now in a covenant relationship with the Living God! He has invested the blood of Jesus, the life of his son, into your growth! You're in good hands! He will never leave, forsake, or abandon you. He will not wait for you to figure it all out by yourself. God is a faithful Shepherd, a loving Father, and a wonderful Gardener! As you grow in your understanding of God's design for your spiritual growth, you will discover that growing up into salvation is indeed a joyful journey.

GLOSSARY *of* TERMS

God the Father—Head of the Trinity, Creator, Judge, Preserver of all things.

Jesus Christ—God the Son who became incarnate to die and raise from the grave for the sins of humanity, eternally one with the trinity.

Holy Spirit—The third person of the trinity, active in the earth through empowerment and gifts to men. He is God with us and in us.

Ordinances—A decree; a prescribed religious rite.

Water baptism—A symbolic practice of publicly expressing faith in Christ through being lowered and raised from the water, as in resurrection.

Communion—The practice of taking bread and wine as symbols of Christ's body and blood, done in remembrance of His sacrifice on the cross.

Intimacy with God—Developing a Father/child relationship with God; a deep bond that goes beyond surface engagement.

Quiet time—Regular appointed time to keep with God, blocking out the rest of the world.

The Voice of God—Communication from God to people through the Bible, a quiet internal voice, or even dreams and visions.

Secret Place—A place of quiet and continual fellowship with the Father.

Worship—The act of expressing reverence, submission, and adoration for God.

Prayer—An address to God in word or thought.

Thanksgiving—An expression of gratitude toward God.

Praise—An expression of admiration and celebration to God.

Intercession—Prayer that is on behalf of another person.

Gifts of the Spirit—Graces given to the church defined in 1 Corinthians 12 that pertain to knowledge, speech and power, which includes: the word of knowledge, the word of wisdom, the discernment of spirits, prophecy, diverse tongues, interpretation of tongues, gifts of healing, miracles, and the gift of faith.

Evangelism—Refers to the propagation of the gospel through the local church and beyond.

Sharing the Gospel—A primary function of evangelism which is to communicate the message of Christ with others.

ABOUT *the* AUTHOR

PETER K. LOUIS and his wife, Kristi, live in Dallas, Texas with their five children. He is the founder of *Braveheart*, a gospel-centered ministry focused on strengthening the faith of the Church and equipping the Body of Christ to walk in love and Christlikeness. Peter enjoys spending time with his family, golfing, fishing and one day dreams of living on a farm.

For more information on *Peter Louis* and *Braveheart*, visit:

BRAVEHEART.RUN

ALSO BY PETER K. LOUIS:

BACK TO THE GOSPEL
Reviving the Church through the Message that Birthed It

BACK TO PENTECOST
Awakening the Church to the Spirit that Launched It

KEEP THE BLOOD WARM
A 30 Day Guide to a Heart on Fire

Made in the USA
Monee, IL
11 May 2022